The Parable of the Talents

Matthew 25:14–30
for children

Written by Nicole E. Dreyer
Illustrated by Susan Morris

CONCORDIA PUBLISHING HOUSE · SAINT LOUIS

Jesus was resting on the Olive Mount
Near the end of His ministry,
When the disciples privately asked their Lord
What the signs of His return would be.

Jesus replied to them, "Keep watch!
You do not know the day."
And then He told them of a man
Who was preparing to go away.
This man was rich, our Savior said,

With wealth and property.
So he gave this order to his men:
"Take care of my talents for me."

The master divided his talents among
Three servants he'd asked to see,
And gave each one a portion of wealth
According to ability.

The first servant called was given five,
The second was given just two,
One for the third. Then their master declared,
"These eight talents I entrust to you."

The master left and Servant One
Said, "I know just what I'll do
I'll put my talents right to work;
To my master I will be true."

Servant Two did exactly the same
And put his two talents to work:
"I'll honor my master's faith and trust;
My duty I will not shirk."

But Servant Three made a foolish choice:
He went home and dug a hole!
"I'll put this deep into the ground
And keep his talent whole."

A long time passed 'til the master returned
And called his servants again
To collect his property and his wealth
And to settle accounts with them

Servant One showed his master that
He'd turned five talents into ten.
The Second returned not two, but four,
And their master was proud of them.

"Well done, my good and faithful men,
You've done what I expected of you—
Now come and enjoy my happiness
And command many instead of few."

But Servant Three now stood before
The master he knew was hard,
And handed back the talent he had
Only buried outside in his yard.

The master was angry when he saw
What the lazy servant had done.
"Throw him out!" the master roared,
"Give his talent to Servant One!"

Jesus, the Master, has given to us
Abilities He wants us to use.
Each one of us has special gifts;
Which talents belong to you?

Maybe you sing or draw or write
Or could it be that you like to act?
Science and history might be your thing,
Or perhaps you are good at math!

Whatever our gifts that Jesus has given
Here's what He has in store:
When we use our talents to honor Him,
He will bless them and give us more.

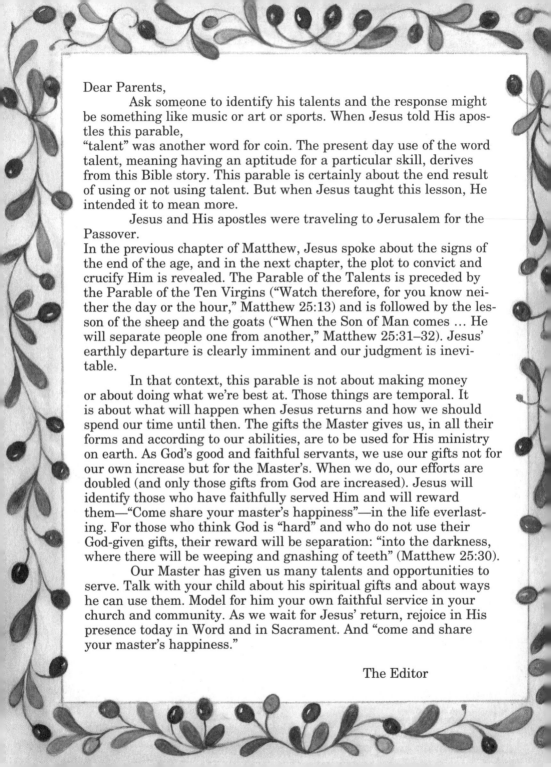

Dear Parents,

Ask someone to identify his talents and the response might be something like music or art or sports. When Jesus told His apostles this parable, "talent" was another word for coin. The present day use of the word talent, meaning having an aptitude for a particular skill, derives from this Bible story. This parable is certainly about the end result of using or not using talent. But when Jesus taught this lesson, He intended it to mean more.

Jesus and His apostles were traveling to Jerusalem for the Passover.
In the previous chapter of Matthew, Jesus spoke about the signs of the end of the age, and in the next chapter, the plot to convict and crucify Him is revealed. The Parable of the Talents is preceded by the Parable of the Ten Virgins ("Watch therefore, for you know neither the day or the hour," Matthew 25:13) and is followed by the lesson of the sheep and the goats ("When the Son of Man comes … He will separate people one from another," Matthew 25:31–32). Jesus' earthly departure is clearly imminent and our judgment is inevitable.

In that context, this parable is not about making money or about doing what we're best at. Those things are temporal. It is about what will happen when Jesus returns and how we should spend our time until then. The gifts the Master gives us, in all their forms and according to our abilities, are to be used for His ministry on earth. As God's good and faithful servants, we use our gifts not for our own increase but for the Master's. When we do, our efforts are doubled (and only those gifts from God are increased). Jesus will identify those who have faithfully served Him and will reward them—"Come share your master's happiness"—in the life everlasting. For those who think God is "hard" and who do not use their God-given gifts, their reward will be separation: "into the darkness, where there will be weeping and gnashing of teeth" (Matthew 25:30).

Our Master has given us many talents and opportunities to serve. Talk with your child about his spiritual gifts and about ways he can use them. Model for him your own faithful service in your church and community. As we wait for Jesus' return, rejoice in His presence today in Word and in Sacrament. And "come and share your master's happiness."

The Editor